Photo by Joan Marcus

A scene from the Manhattan Class Company production of "Nixon's Nixon." Set design by Kyle Chepulis.

NIXON'S NIXON

<small>BY</small> RUSSELL LEES

★

DRAMATISTS
PLAY SERVICE
INC.

NIXON'S NIXON received its premiere at Manhattan Class Company (Robert LuPone and Bernard Telsey, Executive Directors; W.D. Cantler, Associate Director), in New York City, on September 29, 1995. The production was subsequently produced at the Westside Theatre in New York City, by the Shubert Organization, Capital Cities/ABC, Jujamcyn Theaters, and Robert LuPone and Bernard Telsey, on March 5, 1996. It was directed by Jim Simpson; the administrative director was Lynne McCreary; the set and lighting designs were by Kyle Chepulis; the costume design was by Daniele Hollywood; the sound design was by Mike Nolan; casting was by Bernard Telsey Casting; the general manager was Albert Poland; the production supervisors were Laura Kravets Gautier and Ira Mont; the production stage manager was Erica Blum; the assistant stage managers were Ahri Birnbaum, Bernadette McGay and Corry Oullette; and the press representative was Merle Frimark. The cast was as follows:

RICHARD M. NIXON.. Gerry Bamman
HENRY KISSINGER .... Steve Mellor

CHARACTERS

PRESIDENT RICHARD NIXON

SECRETARY OF STATE HENRY KISSINGER

SETTING

August 7, 1974. 10:00 P.M. The Lincoln Sitting Room in the White House. This is President Nixon's favorite room. He often retires here to listen to classical music or hold informal chats with members of his family or staff. It's a cozy retreat with a marble fireplace, a writing table with telephone, Victorian chairs, an ottoman, a high-armed sofa, a stereo with shelves of classical albums, as well as 19th century prints of Lincoln with his family.

This play is a work of fiction.

The events depicted and the dialogue included in this play are in no way intended to represent actual actions or opinions of either Richard Nixon or Henry Kissinger.

AUTHOR'S NOTE

It's a historical fact that the night before Richard Nixon announced his resignation from the Presidency, he summoned Henry Kissinger to meet with him. What happened that storied evening has been the subject of conjecture and dispute ever since. This play gives my version.

Whether the actors physically resemble the historical Nixon and Kissinger isn't particularly important. In fact, too close a resemblance may work against the play, as it raises expectations of parody. For the original New York production, the actors subtly evoked the two men through voice and gesture while not resembling them much at all. Two different actors at one early reading made absolutely no attempt to even sound like the famous pair. During the discussion, the audience agreed that this worked perfectly well, although they would have preferred an accent for Kissinger.

I mention this to emphasize that the play is not so much about historical personages and their character traits as it is about the very human and personal struggles involved in retaining or relinquishing great power and coming to terms with one's legacy.

R.L.

NIXON'S NIXON

At rise: President Nixon is listening to Tchaikovsky's "Fifth Symphony."* He conducts with passion using some rolled-up transcripts as a baton. The music is too loud, such that we can barely hear knocking at the door.

KISSINGER.   Mr. President?... Mr. President? *(He enters dressed in a tuxedo and raincoat, as if called away from a social occasion.)* Mr. President?

NIXON.   Henry! Good to see you.

KISSINGER.   Mr. President?

NIXON.   Sit. Sit, sit. How've you been, Henry? Long time no see.

KISSINGER.   This Mideast business — it's, I, I apologize.

NIXON.   No. No, no. I'm not, it isn't, I'm not. It's good to see you.

KISSINGER.   Yes, sir.

NIXON.   It's good you came.

KISSINGER.   Of course I came, sir. As I say, I've been busy, or I, in this difficult time…. Could we turn down the volume?

NIXON.   Why?

KISSINGER.   It's a bit …

NIXON.   A bit?

KISSINGER.   A bit …

NIXON.   Oh. Yes, yes. Turn it down for God's sake. Can't hear yourself think. *(Nixon sets down baton of papers, then is careful to turn them face down.)*

KISSINGER.   *(With concern.)* How are you?

NIXON.   I'm well. Really very well.

KISSINGER.   Good. I … as I say, it's a difficult time…. Well. Perhaps we should discuss what Ford might do.

NIXON.   I'm light as a feather, almost giddy.

KISSINGER.   Yes. Good. I'm a little concerned about —

---

* See Special Note on Songs and Recordings on copyright page.

7

NIXON. Maybe it's the music. The spirit soars.

KISSINGER. I worried you'd be depressed.

NIXON. Died penniless, you know. A pauper. Great man like that. Ended up in the shit can.

KISSINGER. Tchaikovsky?

NIXON. Such are the vagaries of history.

KISSINGER. Tchaikovsky died a wealthy man.

NIXON. Few men can control their own destiny, Henry. Only the truly great.

KISSINGER. I'm glad you're taking this so philosophically. *(Pause.)*

NIXON. Taking what so philosophically?

KISSINGER. The…. Your … I understood you'd …

NIXON. Ron issued a schedule. You know that? A resignation schedule. Gave copies to Haig, Buchanan. I'm not supposed to know about it. I might react badly. It might influence my decision.

KISSINGER. Mm. *(Pause.)* So you haven't decided?

NIXON. 1958. Ike sends me on some functionary trip, some dull figure-head thing. South America. Caracas. July. Anti-American mobs surround the car. They're this far away from me, Henry. You're me. They're this far. Screaming. Pig-dog! Imperialist murderer! Stuff like that. Capitalist-piece-of-shit!! With bats, sticks, banging on the car. BAM! BAM! They want to rip my dick off and shove it down my throat.

KISSINGER. Sir.

NIXON. So what do I do? What would you do, Doctor Kissinger? Ingratiate yourself with a quip? Negotiate your way out?

KISSINGER. Mr. President.

NIXON. They're banging on the car! They're shattering the windows! Pig shit!! Now, Henry, when confronting a mob, always do the unexpected. Me, I get out of the car. I get out of the car! Unexpected? They're stunned. Flabbergasted. A mass of dirty faces. Fierce bad teeth. I shake a couple of hands. How about that, Henry? I even shake a couple of hands. It's a campaign stop.

KISSINGER. It's a wonderful story. I think, however, the lesson to be learned —

NIXON. Overnight, I'm a hero.

KISSINGER. — is a lesson of courage, not recklessness.

NIXON. Courage. You're right. Courage. How did I win them over? Latin countries, courage is the thing. Balls. They love a guy with balls. Cojones. That's why you have so much trouble with them. In America it's a little different. Americans like fighters. Underdogs. The scrappier the better. That's me, now. Me. I'm the underdog. Everyone's deserted me. Now I'm the guy to root for. *(He goes into a kind of trance.)*

KISSINGER. Mr. President?

NIXON. So? You see?

KISSINGER. I don't see.

NIXON. I'm the guy to root for.

KISSINGER. Root for? Root for to do what?

NIXON. I've always come back. Every time I've been counted out, I've come back. The governor's race. The Hiss thing. Even when Ike screwed me over.

KISSINGER. This is not when Ike screwed you over.

NIXON. I've always come back.

KISSINGER. Sir.

NIXON. Always.

KISSINGER. This time ...

NIXON. Haldeman, gone. Ehrlichman. My administration in shambles.

KISSINGER. The Senate, it's been clear for some time, they simply aren't —

NIXON. ... Colson, Mitchell ...

KISSINGER. — aren't going to rally behind you.

NIXON. Dean lying like a weasel. Goddamn. Mngh. Cocksucker.

KISSINGER. Mr. President, will you listen? Impeachment is certain.

NIXON. I'm alone.

KISSINGER. Impeachment and conviction.

NIXON. Impeachment? Conviction?! Know how many fat congressional butts I've — screw impeachment. Screw the Senators. Sheep. Candy ass sheep. I get a ground swell, they'll

9

follow like ducks.

KISSINGER. Ducks? Ducks? Will you look around?

NIXON. Mnh!

KISSINGER. Everyone's quit, fired, indicted. It's a tragedy. But you must, we all must come to terms with it.

NIXON. All my advisors, you're the only one. The only one who's escaped.

KISSINGER. That's hardly —

NIXON. Even the wiretap thing, the press backed off. You threaten to resign, they collapse. Me, they're licking their chops.

KISSINGER. I've suffered from the press. I'm sure they'd be overjoyed if I —

NIXON. No. It's true. You they still respect. Of course, they're Jews, most of them.

KISSINGER. Sir, you don't think I've ever — has someone said? I mean, I have good relations with the press. But I have never, never used that to hurt you.

NIXON. Somebody around here sold me out, you know.

KISSINGER. I know.

NIXON. Was it you?

KISSINGER. Mr. President, I've just explained —

NIXON. I didn't think so. But I wanted to hear it from you.

KISSINGER. It would be crazy.

NIXON. Who was it?

KISSINGER. I have no idea.

NIXON. It's somebody.

KISSINGER. Yes, but who?

NIXON. You don't know?

KISSINGER. Absolutely not.

NIXON. No idea?

KISSINGER. None.

NIXON. Someday I'll find out. Things can't be kept secret forever you know.

KISSINGER. *(Pause.)* Frankly, I figured it must be Haig.

NIXON. Haig?

KISSINGER. Well. It makes sense —

NIXON. Haig?

KISSINGER. He's the one who —

NIXON. The one man who's stood by me? The one man I can confide in?

KISSINGER. But that's my point.

NIXON. I can't believe you just impugned General Alexander Haig.

KISSINGER. It's merely speculation, based on —

NIXON. Because I listen to his advice.

KISSINGER. I respect Haig. I absolutely respect Haig. He and I, we've ... What's he say about me?

NIXON. What do you mean, "What's he say about me?"

KISSINGER. It's just that in a bureaucracy it's tempting to ... back stab. I've seen him do it to others.

NIXON. What does he say about me?

KISSINGER. Haig? He's respectful. But he can ... he likes to imitate people.

NIXON. I see.

KISSINGER. No, but he's, generally ... Perfectly correct.

NIXON. Yes. Yes. Does *he* want me to resign? Probably does, but he won't come out and say so.

KISSINGER. Mr. President, it's time to make the decision conclusively. This, this cloud hanging over you, it's —

NIXON. Cloud.

KISSINGER. More than a cloud, yes. It's —

NIXON. We had our successes, we two. Not so long ago.

KISSINGER. We did. And, if permitted, I will continue —

NIXON. China. Russia. Should be worth something.

KISSINGER. The world is a safer place.

NIXON. Don't give me your platitudes. Haig. Haig, for one, has stood by me. Not like you. Compare what you've done for me to anybody, compare it to Julie. My family, *Julie's* been the one, Pat and Tricia too, sure, but Julie's the one gave all those speeches. Went all over the place y'know. Hecklers and everything.

KISSINGER. Yes.

NIXON. They booed her, you know. Sometimes.

KISSINGER. I wondered how you.

NIXON. What?

KISSINGER. ... how you ... were able to permit —

NIXON. How I let her do that?

KISSINGER. She put herself in an awfully vulnerable position. *(Nixon thinks hard.)* I'm sorry, I.

NIXON. No. It's, um. *(He thinks hard some more, then, abruptly.)* Think Brezhnev'll get along with Jerry like he did me?

KISSINGER. So you *have* — You are going to, um, pass the baton.

NIXON. He won't.

KISSINGER. Jerry? With Brezhnev? No. No, he won't.

NIXON. Leonid and I ...

KISSINGER. Yes ... yes ...

NIXON. He, he respects me.

KISSINGER. Yes. Of course he did. Certainly.

NIXON. Yes, he does. He, for one, does. You be him.

KISSINGER. Him?

NIXON. I'll be me.

KISSINGER. ...

NIXON. The Moscow summit.

KISSINGER. Sir ...

NIXON. Will you just be him? Jesus. Okay, I'll be him, you be me. Nixon! Good to meet you!

KISSINGER. ...

NIXON-AS-BREZHNEV. Nixon! Good to meet you!

KISSINGER. ...

NIXON. For God's sake, do this one thing for me. Jesus-fuckin'-Christ!... *(As Brezhnev.)* Nixon!

KISSINGER-AS-NIXON. Premier Brezhnev. A great pleasure.

NIXON-AS-BREZHNEV. Please, please call me Leonid. But this is historic! *(Grabs Kissinger and hugs him.)* Yes. You are a strong man. A sturdy man.

KISSINGER-AS-NIXON. You are a sturdy man as well.

NIXON-AS-BREZHNEV. I feel we will accomplish much, my friend. We share a great deal.

KISSINGER-AS-NIXON. Oh?

NIXON-AS-BREZHNEV. We are simple men. Family men. Ah, but there ... You love politics — your daughter marries a President's grandson. I love circuses, my daughter runs off with

12

lion tamers, acrobats. We both love our daughters, but yours has brought you joy. Mine has brought me pain.

KISSINGER-AS-NIXON. I've been lucky.

NIXON-AS-BREZHNEV. You see. I've studied you closely. The KGB files, ah! again and again I've read them. I know you like I've known no lover. *(Big Soviet laugh. Kissinger checks his watch.)* We have both overcome adversity to become ... what?

KISSINGER. ...

NIXON-AS-BREZHNEV. Born to simple, working people we have succeeded in becoming —

KISSINGER-AS-NIXON. Middle class. *(A look from Nixon.)* The most powerful men in the world.

NIXON-AS-BREZHNEV. Yes. Yes, you have it exactly. With intelligent minions to scamper about for us. But here we've been chatting and forgotten the primary thing. Vodka! First quality Russian vodka! *(He gets a decanter of brandy.)* Will you please join me?

KISSINGER-AS-NIXON. I believe I will.

NIXON-AS-BREZHNEV. *(Pouring brandy.)* So, Nixon. Tell me a bit about this Kissinger.

KISSINGER-AS-NIXON. He ... he and I have a ...

NIXON-AS-BREZHNEV. I get the feeling you're not very close.

KISSINGER-AS-NIXON. ... I suppose not.... We discuss things. In depth. He's more than an advisor. Much, much more.

NIXON-AS-BREZHNEV. Knowledgeable about history, I'm told.

KISSINGER-AS-NIXON. Astonishingly knowledgeable.

NIXON-AS-BREZHNEV. Tell me, Nixon, do you contemplate what the history books will make of you? Do you wonder about your place in history?

KISSINGER-AS-NIXON. A statesman can't occupy himself —

NIXON-AS-BREZHNEV. Of course you do. And it will be a glorious place, I'm certain. *(As himself.)* This is wonderful. You be Brezhnev now. Just for a minute.... Go ahead.

KISSINGER-AS-BREZHNEV. *(Drinks.)* But, Nixon, you must be careful. We have just this minute met and I already have advantage over you.

NIXON. You think so?

KISSINGER-AS-BREZHNEV. It's of little consequence. Each of us will gain and lose advantages in due course.

NIXON. What have you won here?

KISSINGER-AS-BREZHNEV. You are concerned with the history books. It's a weakness, Nixon. Me, I have no such concern.

NIXON. Very good.

KISSINGER-AS-BREZHNEV. This gives me leverage in our dealings.

NIXON. You're right.

KISSINGER-AS-BREZHNEV. And I shall use it, Nixon. I shall squeeze you until you're bloody.

NIXON. I'm certain you will.

KISSINGER-AS-BREZHNEV. *(Parody of big Soviet laugh.)* Perhaps a little more Vodka.

NIXON. I have an advantage, too.

KISSINGER-AS-BREZHNEV. Yes?

NIXON. I have more nuclear submarines. 'Course, Kissinger nearly threw that away.... Well? You did screw up on the submarines. But we got around it. We were out in uncharted territory. Mistakes were bound to happen, but we fudged 'em. That's our genius. History. That's where the big judgments are. You think history books're going to say, "He didn't do his homework on submarines?" No. It's boring. It's piddly-ass. "He got the first nuclear arms treaty!" That's good reading. Good history.

KISSINGER. Mm.

NIXON. Which gets to the heart of it, doesn't it? What do you think, Henry? What'll they say about me in a hundred years?

KISSINGER. You?

NIXON. What will be the verdict?

KISSINGER. You.... You'll be treated well enough, I'm sure. Yes. We've accomplished many remarkable things.

NIXON. You think so?

KISSINGER. Oh, yes.

NIXON. I'll be well treated?

KISSINGER. China alone.

NIXON. Mm.

KISSINGER. Mm. *(Pause.)*

NIXON. They'll discount the piddly stuff.

KISSINGER. Historians will look back bewildered.

NIXON. Jefferson had some funny business, didn't he?

KISSINGER. I'm sure he did.

NIXON. He did all right. What about Lincoln, didn't he have some...? No?

KISSINGER. Lincoln, no.

NIXON. Crazy wife.

KISSINGER. Yes, but —

NIXON. What about Grant? He as crummy as all that?

KISSINGER. I think, yes, he was less than —

NIXON. What I mean is, the bad ones, were they that bad, or is it all press?

KISSINGER. The bad ones. The good ones. What is important is the place you hold. History recognizes the trivial for just that.

NIXON. The big stuff'll stand the test of ... yes.

KISSINGER. But, my point is, that is only if our projects are carried to fruition.

NIXON. Our projects. The big picture stuff. People don't understand.

KISSINGER. For this, it's important that Ford understand how essential it is that I remain Secretary of State.

NIXON. And god knows what.... All the rotten stuff we came up with here. Good Lord. That's what I'm worried about.

KISSINGER. That...?

NIXON. That every little thing'll come out.

KISSINGER. Of course not.

NIXON. Because of the tapes, see. The tapes. They're making a big deal about 'em.

KISSINGER. Well, yes.

NIXON. I must've listened to those damn tapes, ... it's enough to ... god. "There's a cancer on the Presidency." Jesus.

KISSINGER. You shouldn't have gotten caught up in them.

You neglected —

NIXON. You're on 'em, too, you know. There's bad tapes with you on there.

KISSINGER. I suppose.

NIXON. There aren't any tapes of Lincoln saying bad stuff. He did. Any man, this office, has to consider all kinds of, but I'm the one everybody wants to hear the tapes. If I'm President, if I'm President in good standing, with no impeachment crap, I'm okay. The tapes are mine, I can throw away the crummy ones.

KISSINGER. What conversations were...?

NIXON. But now, the way things are, that's destroying evidence. If I'm under indictment, I can't, can't ...

KISSINGER. Exercise your prerogative.

NIXON. No. My hands're ... you see?

KISSINGER. It's a problem.

NIXON. They're my goddamn tapes.

KISSINGER. Right.

NIXON. Like a diary. Like a Presidential diary.

KISSINGER. Which ones have negative things about me?

NIXON. Good god, which ones don't? Pakistan, Cuba, Chile for chrissakes, Christmas bombings. It's all through there.

KISSINGER. That's on tape?

NIXON. ...

KISSINGER. Those conversations were taped?

NIXON. Don't you get it? Everything was.

KISSINGER. But those were, I wasn't informed of, nobody has access to those.

NIXON. Access, no. Nobody has access. Of course not. You think I'm crazy?

KISSINGER. They're locked up.

NIXON. You bet they're locked up.

KISSINGER. They don't have any bearing on —

NIXON. No. You're safe for godsakes. Executive privilege up the wazoo.

KISSINGER. No one has access.

NIXON. No one has access. No one has excess. Excrete, escape, exculpatory. Ex, ex, ex, ex-president. Historians?! What do they know? *(Pause.)*

KISSINGER. I just want to be clear. No one can listen to those tapes.

NIXON. No. As long as they aren't subpoenaed.

KISSINGER. And there's no reason for that.

NIXON. Right.

KISSINGER. And there won't be.

NIXON. No. No, why should there?

KISSINGER. Because it's separate.

NIXON. Right.

KISSINGER. Good.... Good.

NIXON. So as long as I keep them locked up, I'll be seen as, as ...

KISSINGER. Once you have ... left office, your legacy in the field of foreign affairs, of course, will —

NIXON. Oh god, yes. Brezhnev was practically a brother. Not like those European sad sacks. Pompidou? My god. Sits around the Elysee Palace like a big cold turd. Willie Brandt. Germans are all Nazis, don't understand why they pretend any different. The thing about history is it's a bunch of crock.

KISSINGER. Mmm-yes. However, the best way to preserve your place is to gracefully —

NIXON. I mean look at Lincoln here. I mean, yeah, there's a lot of, he wasn't, but underneath all that, *underneath,* he was a real guy. He sat in this goddamned chair. He sat here, and he ruled this country. As I have. Henry. Just a regular guy, caught in a very difficult ... time.

KISSINGER. Sir.

NIXON. Yes?

KISSINGER. We have to talk about your decision.

NIXON. I'm all ears.

KISSINGER. The country, our country has yet to heal from the war. And now we're plunged into this, this domestic crisis. Right or wrong. We're plunged into it and there's no solution that can bring all the camps together, that can unify this country once again. And, sir, if there's anything you've stood for it's the strength and unity of purpose of this nation. *(Pause.)*

17

NIXON.   I grew up stacking groceries. I grew up spraying vegetables, picking spiders out of the bananas. My hands still stink of pesticide. Those were tough years.

KISSINGER.   In the present situation you've defended yourself well. You've defended yourself honorably. But it's dragged on too long. It's ripping apart the White House, it's ripping apart the country.

NIXON.   Worked pumping gas. Worked mimeographing legal crap. Worked for everything I've ever had.

KISSINGER.   I really think the best thing for you personally, for your family, for Julie, for the nation, is for you to definitively step down and let me carry out our program.

NIXON.   I didn't grow up on some aristocratic German estate.

KISSINGER.   You are, finally ...

NIXON.   Pampered and coddled like a Prussian prince.

KISSINGER.   ... I beg your pardon?

NIXON.   Handed a meal ticket to the Ivy League.

KISSINGER.   My father was a schoolteacher. I went to college on the GI bill.

NIXON.   Don't play sob-sister with me.

KISSINGER.   I owe a great deal to this country.

NIXON.   My god yes. A great debt of loyalty.

KISSINGER.   As a matter of fact.

NIXON.   Well, we all do. I've always sought to, everything I've done, even my own interest, I've always sought first to honor.... I've worked so.... At night I go over, that's when. Fickle. The thing of it is, Henry, people elect you, they have high expectations. Christ, did they ever elect me! What a landslide! I appeal to the Richard Nixon in everybody. So they're all jam-packed full of hope and elation. They, there's no way to. They expect so much ... and what happens is you're the leader, you're sure to ... disappoint. So, they want to get rid of you. Get some new.... Even you want me to get out of the way. Of course you do. That brandy there? That's the brandy we toasted the China breakthrough with. Would you please? *(Kissinger pours brandies. They drink.)* We've toasted success in this room. Days gone by. Many, many triumphs.

KISSINGER.   Yes. This room holds fine memories for me.

NIXON.   The protests. Huh? We sat here. Thank god we had the brandy then. Will they put me in jail? *(Pause.)*

KISSINGER.   I can't imagine such a thing.

NIXON.   They might. I might go to jail.... So what. Huh, Henry? So what? This century's greatest political writing's been done in jail.

KISSINGER.   Yes, Castro. Lenin.

NIXON.   I was thinking Sakharov and Gandhi.

KISSINGER.   ... Gandhi.

NIXON.   The thing of it is, if I'm convicted, I lose my pension.... I've looked into it. I lose my pension and Secret Service protection.

KISSINGER.   I, I really don't think you'll come to trial.

NIXON.   Nope. I'd lose the, uh ... I mean in addition to the ...

KISSINGER.   You. I really think.

NIXON.   But who cares now? *(Pause.)* Depends on Jerry.

KISSINGER.   I'm sure he'll —

NIXON.   Have you heard any...?

KISSINGER.   No.

NIXON.   He's a good man.

KISSINGER.   He's a good and decent man.

NIXON.   He'll...?

KISSINGER.   He'll see that you're ... *(Pause.)*

NIXON.   Brought to this, what more could they do? What's left? I've been run over by a tank.

KISSINGER.   It's true.

NIXON.   I'm the guy who came to the party and peed in the lemonade.

KISSINGER.   Now they're out to get you.

NIXON.   They've gotten me.

KISSINGER.   Conspired against you.

NIXON.   Picked me clean. Might as well strip myself naked.

KISSINGER.   Might as well.

NIXON.   March down Pennsylvania Avenue.

KISSINGER.   With a band.

NIXON.   Flopping all over the place.

KISSINGER. A band and bunting.

NIXON. Baloop, baloop! And it all goes down the drain. China. Detente. Arms pacts. Viet Nam. *That's* the.

KISSINGER. It won't go down the drain if Ford keeps me on with full authority —

NIXON. We did the right thing there, Henry.

KISSINGER. — full authority to. Where?

NIXON. Viet Nam.

KISSINGER. Oh. Yes.

NIXON. It was, it was a tough. Those cocksuckers! Thought they could, and the, the goddamn.... We did the right — you won the goddamn prize for chrissake!

KISSINGER. We —

NIXON. So, yes. I mean, it was about boys, men slogging around in a jungle. My god, can you imagine? At night, in the mud, so far from home, all on your own. Your buddy's guts dripping from the trees. Enemies. Everywhere, enemies.

KISSINGER. Enemies there *and* here.

NIXON. Oh god. Jesus-God, Henry! My god. *(Pause.)* You'd think it was a crime, what I did. You'd think getting us out was a crime. We were tearing our hair out.

KISSINGER. The options were so ...

NIXON. Boys died. Yes. Boys died. You're President, that's part of the. Good god, look at the body count in the Civil War! Lots more than, and he's on Mount Rushmore.

KISSINGER. You got us out.

NIXON. Henry, I said, I called you into my office, Henry, I said, close the door.

KISSINGER. Le Duc Tho won't budge. They're flaunting their disdain.

NIXON. Little faggot.

KISSINGER. We need a credible threat.

NIXON. Tell 'em we'll, by god we'll ...

KISSINGER. They're sophisticated. They hector me about domestic opposition.

NIXON. You know how Ike won Korea? Do you know? He threatened nuclear.

KISSINGER. Yes, but we —

NIXON.   He threatened nuclear and they were in negotiating like somebody shoved an electric —

KISSINGER.   Eisenhower had nuclear dominance. We don't.

NIXON.   Can't we threaten it?

KISSINGER.   The problem is we're fighting on two fronts. If we even mention nuclear —

NIXON.   The beardos and weirdoes go berserk.

KISSINGER.   Right. We must avoid stirring up domestic opposition.

NIXON.   We can't make our toughest threat.

KISSINGER.   One approach, how would we do this?

NIXON.   We'd have to.

KISSINGER.   Is to convince the North somehow that we might go nuclear.

NIXON.   Damn the consequences?

KISSINGER.   In a way. It's irrational, but we could convince them that you're, well, not rational ...

NIXON.   This is for the nuclear thing?

KISSINGER.   Yes. We convince them —

NIXON.   I see.

KISSINGER.   That the war's made you desperate —

NIXON.   — and maybe a little unhinged. Uh-huh.

KISSINGER.   Yes. They might believe you're willing to risk nuclear war with the Soviets.

NIXON.   Whichever side wins, North Vietnam'd be a cinder.

KISSINGER.   Right.

NIXON.   Right. Convince them I'm a little funny.

KISSINGER.   Right. But domestically ...

NIXON.   Domestically, we're screwed. We'd have to do it secret. I'd have to *secretly* be off my rocker.

KISSINGER.   How we'd manage that ...

NIXON.   We'd have to actually do something, I think.

KISSINGER.   I agree. We must take some action implying you're ...

NIXON.   Right. We can't, you know, write Ho Chi Minh a letter saying, "Nixon's a banana." We've got to get him to figure it out.

KISSINGER.   All right. How about this? The army's been after us about Cambodia. Well, what can we do? It's a neutral country. The Viet Cong aren't supposed to be there, but neither are we. We can't go after them. We can't just go and invade a neutral country.

NIXON.   We can't?

KISSINGER.   It'd be expanding a war we want to end. But. If we could get the V.C. headquarters hiding there, it'd cripple them. It's a vast jungle, we'd have to bomb the hell out of it. We'd have to follow up with ground troops.

NIXON.   Bomb the hell out of it. And the peaceniks?

KISSINGER.   We'd keep it secret.

NIXON.   The whole thing?

KISSINGER.   Yes.

NIXON.   We'd bomb the bejesus out of Cambodia, send in ground troops, and keep the whole operation secret?

KISSINGER.   Right.

NIXON.   This is good, Henry. This is very good.

KISSINGER.   We can't tell most of the army. We'll have to pick officers and units. We'll have to skip over several links in the chain of command.

NIXON.   What about Sihanouk? He could screw us. I mean, we're bombing his country, he's bound to find out.

KISSINGER.   He's in a tricky position. The Viet Cong are in his jungle. He can't complain we're bombing them unless he admits they're there. I think he'll shut up and try to please everyone.

NIXON.   Yes. What about, I suppose the Cambodians ...

KISSINGER.   Those villages are completely isolated. Reports of destruction will be incoherent.

NIXON.   Henry! This is a masterstroke. It's bold, daring, sweeping. It gets at those bastards without hurting us at home. Plus, it conveys to Hanoi they're dealing with someone capable of anything! It holds a subtle but distinct tinge of madness.

KISSINGER.   Thank you.

NIXON.   *(In present.)* Ah. Might've worked. Eventually. Hadn't leaked out. *(He pours another brandy.)* Ike and I used to chat here. As much as we ever chatted.

KISSINGER.   When he wasn't golfing?

NIXON.   He only won World War II for chrissake. And Korea. He was a father figure to me, a wonderful, he taught me goddamn fly-fishing.... God, what he put me through in '52. I would've done, I worshipped, every two days I had to prove myself. Goddamn *cocksucker*. A drag on the ticket! Fuck him. I helped the ticket. I helped the ticket both times. I would've been President myself in '60, Kennedy hadn't've cheated. Kennedy. If he could, he'd've cheated his way into getting elected Pope. Smuggling Marilyn into the Vatican chambers. Hell, I'd make twice the Pope he would've. How 'bout that, Henry? Me, Pope? Jesus God, I'd grab the world by the tits and give it a whirl.

KISSINGER.   You'd make an excellent Pope.

NIXON.   Because once you're elected, you're *it*. You're Pope till you die.

KISSINGER.   I don't think I'd have much chance at Pope.

NIXON.   Anybody could pull it off, this goes back to the Kennedy thing, as long as you can act the part. I don't think Pope John really, I mean, he's okay. Kennedy taught me something there. He was one great actor. Debates? I beat his balls off. Ask anybody. He acted his way to President.

KISSINGER.   You have to be an actor.

NIXON.   God, yes. This job, you have to be. On the world stage and so on.

KISSINGER.   The press. To be properly duplicitous —

NIXON.   You've got to portray ... you've got to believe —

KISSINGER.   The true statesman, he's a chameleon. He shades his opinions, even facts, to draw in and seduce his opponents. Occasionally, I even convince myself.

NIXON.   It's more than that, Henry. It's that ... the burdens of the position. If you show your true self, you're standing there with your fly wide open. If you show your true self, your weaknesses are all ...

KISSINGER.   You've got to wear the proper Greek mask.

NIXON.   Yes.

KISSINGER.   You've got to be larger than life.

NIXON.   That's it exactly. Because you've got to play the great man of state. You've got to play the wise leader, the brilliant schemer. The ruthless murderer. But with no backstage. There's no backstage. The mask gets stuck. You end up asking, "What color are my goddamn eyes?" *(Long pause.)*

KISSINGER.   You will certainly be remembered as a great man unjustly brought down.

NIXON.   You think so?

KISSINGER.   You'll be remembered all the better for the tragedy of your fall.

NIXON.   It is tragic.

KISSINGER.   Because you could have been one of the greats. Alexander, Caesar, Napoleon…. Look how badly the British treated Churchill.

NIXON.   Limey snots.

KISSINGER.   It is for me to carry on.

NIXON.   Napoleon returned from exile, you know. After Russia, he was exiled to some island. He came back after a year or so with a few hundred men. The King of France sent an entire army to stop him. They form a line across the road, rifles at the ready. Bayonets trembling. He halts his troops, Henry. He halts them and walks alone to the front of the column. There he confronts soldiers who'd fought for him for years, now ready to shoot him down. "Men of France! You know who I am." Here he opens his great-coat and stands before them. "Shoot if you must." One of the officers shouts, "Fire!"

KISSINGER.   *(Pause.)* Fire!

NIXON.   Absolute silence. They throw down their muskets, run to embrace their Emperor. They carry him to Paris in triumph. Is that too much to ask?

KISSINGER.   Too much?

NIXON.   Now you say Waterloo. Yes, Waterloo. But by coming back he got that chance. He almost won, he got that chance.

KISSINGER.   You're saying …

NIXON.   I want my chance.

KISSINGER.   Your chance?

NIXON.   I can fight this thing. It isn't over.

KISSINGER.   You'll be *impeached.*

NIXON. Yes, I know. I'll fight it out in the courts.

KISSINGER. No.

NIXON. Pat's for it. My whole family's behind me. Julie, Tricia. Not David.

KISSINGER. You had your chance. What're you trying to do, wreck us? Wreck everything we've done?

NIXON. I'm not gonna —

KISSINGER. You are. Don't you understand? I can't do anything. I can't get an appointment with Dobrynin for god's sake. They're all waiting, the world over, waiting for your body to hit the floor. And here, in Washington? They don't even wait, they're gathering like smiling buzzards, gauging the spoils. Meanwhile, no one will talk to me, they know I can't make commitments until there's a new President. I can't continue my work.

NIXON. Too bad for you.

KISSINGER. Too bad for me? If you're remembered, it'll be for what I did. And it's all coming apart, it's all going to shit because you won't get out of the way. *(Long pause.)* I'm sorry.

NIXON. Who cares what the books say, if the guy on the street, the little guy in Peoria, if he thinks different? Historians. Fuzzy headed clowns in tweed, jerking off in some library. The guy in the street! He thinks Nixon was a bum, then Nixon was a bum, screw historians! How'm I gonna fix that, stewing in my own exiled juice? I can't. I'll go down history a bum.

KISSINGER. You could ... you could write your memoirs.... Perhaps it's a bit soon. Maybe we could set up some sort of consulting position with Jerry.

NIXON. I've thought about that.

KISSINGER. We could, I don't know.

NIXON. It'll be tough to.

KISSINGER. It is perhaps best to wait. Possibly after the '76 election. We could bring you in then.

NIXON. And then, *then* the soldiers will throw down their muskets.

KISSINGER. You'll march into Congress and throw open your great-coat.

NIXON. They'll cheer, they'll cheer me like they did in

Amman. In Cairo. Like they did in Paris, Bonn and London. Like Caracas. Nixon! Nixon! Nixon! They went wild. You got your share, too. Other times. Winning that Nobel thing. Acted like I was the doorman.

KISSINGER. I was careful in my speech to —

NIXON. Nobody listens to that stuff. It's the headlines and the photo in the morning. But no, they loved me at the convention. They loved my State of the Union. Pretty pathetic, sit around here, listing the times I've been cheered. All I've done, I'm counting cheers.

KISSINGER. We're all so fragile.

NIXON. But see, it's the cheers that. Did they really want me? That's what gets me. They seemed to want the hell outta me. If the Kennedys'd lived, would I have ever gotten elected?

KISSINGER. That's quite an interesting question.

NIXON. Say Kennedy gets a second term in '64. Then Bobby in '68, maybe '72. Me in '76.

KISSINGER. They'd have been stuck with Viet Nam.

NIXON. You think they'd've won all those elections? No chance for me?

KISSINGER. I'm saying if.

NIXON. I could've won. Damn near beat John in '60. Sometimes I wonder if I did win. Those damn Democrats, christ! Illinois, people voted fifteen times. Dead people voted. Same thing in Texas, Missouri. I met with him, you know. After the election. Worried I'd contest it, demand a recount. I ever tell you about that meeting?

KISSINGER. Ten, twenty times.

NIXON. He summons me like I'm. I walk in. He's sitting there, rich and presidential, like a cut of veal. I call him 'Mr. President-Elect.' "How the hell do you take Ohio?" he says. He expected to carry Ohio. I want to say, "I didn't steal it, buster." I sit down. I notice him glance at my shoes. My shoes! I swear, a little sneer came across his face. Then he says, you know what he says?

KISSINGER-AS-KENNEDY. The recent election, closely contested as it was, has left the country vulnerable.

NIXON. I have told you this.

KISSINGER-AS-KENNEDY. A divided America is a weakened America.

NIXON. My people tell me I should contest Illinois. They tell me I should contest Texas.

KISSINGER-AS-KENNEDY. The office of the President, Mr. Nixon, is the collective dream of a nation.

NIXON. My people think I have a case.

KISSINGER-AS-KENNEDY. But this is my point, Mr. Nixon. If you raised this hubbub; if you were to contest this or that state, the election is thrown into question. The collective dream would become troubled.

NIXON. I appreciate your position.

KISSINGER-AS-KENNEDY. Let's say you did. Let's suppose you raise this issue. Let us suppose, Mr. Nixon, you took those electoral votes from Illinois. What would you stand to gain? The election goes to the House of Representatives. I think you'll agree that the heavily Democratic House is likely to vote against you.

NIXON. I think that if I can show that I got more than fifty percent of the popular vote and that your party cheated during a Presidential election, I think a lot of Congressmen would look awfully fair-minded by voting for me. Secondly, if I also carried Texas, which I think I did, I win the Presidency outright and your House of Representatives can go fuck themselves.

KISSINGER-AS-KENNEDY. *(Pause.)* Can I have someone bring you a drink, Mr. Nixon? Some lemonade?

NIXON. Thank you, no.

KISSINGER-AS-KENNEDY. I find it hard to believe that you, Mr. Nixon, would gamble the unity of your country for an outside chance at the presidency. You have experience in foreign affairs. You made sure no one forgot *that* during the election. Perhaps, in a few months, I could ask you to take a diplomatic assignment of some kind.

NIXON. He was trying to buy me off! Why not just offer me cash straight up?! You know what I should've done?

KISSINGER. You did precisely —

NIXON. I should've said, "Grab hold of your pedigree, you

sneering snob, 'cause by the time this is over, you'll look like the Prince of Thieves."

KISSINGER.   You did precisely the correct and honorable thing.

NIXON.   Honorable? "Mr. President, I recognize you fully as President blah-blah-blah no intention of questioning blah-blah-bleah!" There is no honor in quitting, Henry. Ever.

KISSINGER.   On the contrary —

NIXON.   You know what he said to me, after I'd yielded?

KISSINGER.   "Mr. Nixon, the President of the United States is grateful for the fine thing you've —"

NIXON.   Ha! "Mr. Nixon, thank you for meeting with me. I think we can both agree, it's for the best you didn't quite make it."

KISSINGER.   Nevertheless.

NIXON.   The one time I didn't fight hammer and claw to the bloody end, and I regretted it for the next eight years.

KISSINGER.   You were able to return at a more propitious time.

NIXON.   There's no returning from this one.

KISSINGER.   But *I* will carry on.

NIXON.   No come back from total disgrace. Maybe things would've gone differently, I'd won in '60. Maybe I'd be all right now … *(Pause.)* It's a ghostly city at night. Peopled by monuments to the dead and a few Secret Service men.

KISSINGER.   So. You understand that, in order to insure —

NIXON.   Yes. You don't have to hit me over the head.

KISSINGER.   But you agree.

NIXON.   Agree to what?

KISSINGER.   Agree that —

NIXON.   Agree I've got to insure my legacy lives on some-how, some way. But what how? What way, Henry? What a fool I am! My legacy will live on in the person of you! Super K! Henry the Great! You will be the womb that carries my brain-child into the future. You, who I dredged out of obscurity, will nurse my fate at your bosom. You and your liberal coddling, starlet-schtupping, press-licking self! My protégé! My Machie-velli with a belly.

KISSINGER. I'm trying to protect your place in history.

NIXON. You're trying to protect *your* place in history.

KISSINGER. It's the same.

NIXON. Oh, no. No. I'm well aware it's not the same.

KISSINGER. Mr. Nixon. I have at all times remained loyal and have done whatever in my power —

NIXON. Have you?

KISSINGER. Yes.

NIXON. Why, I better call Jerry this second. What if he gets it into his head that he's President? He might go mad with power. Hire Haig for State. Oh-ho. That's what this is about. You're worried Ford comes in here, he'll make a clean sweep. Haig's more his kind of guy. You came here to get me to convince Jerry to keep you. Jiminy-christ, where's his phone number? My last act as President should be to protect you — the single one of my advisors who has never once made any attempt to publicly defend me.

KISSINGER. I have to protect my position as a political entity.

NIXON. Presidents may come and Presidents may go, but Henry Kissinger —

KISSINGER. I am trying to prop up a crumbling empire. Who has been President? Who has been President these past months? You? Cocooned in audio tape, intently listening to yourself, trying to discover an inner, more honorable Nixon. Who's been President? I have. Working to prevent Brezhnev, Castro, Sadat from taking advantage of your feebleness. Me. I've had to cover your lapses and drunken absences. Worse, your drunken presence.

NIXON. I am the President! You are Secretary of State. You owe me respect. You owe me honor.

KISSINGER. I owe you nothing. You think I'm self-interested? You self-absorbed, self-pitying sap. *(Nixon throws his drink in Kissinger's face. Pause.)* I'm. I.

NIXON. You're not going?

KISSINGER. Yes, I.

NIXON. No. don't —

KISSINGER. It's become. We've.

NIXON.   No, no. Don't. I.

KISSINGER.   I'm sorry, Mr. President. The.

NIXON.   Henry.

KISSINGER.   Perhaps in the morning.

NIXON.   Don't go, Henry. Don't leave me. Please. *(Pause. Kissinger moves to the Brandy.)* Oh yes. Drinks, by all means. Freshen mine. Freshen mine right up. We'll. I'm, the stress.

KISSINGER.   Yes. Me, too.

NIXON.   I, uh. A drink, yes. You're right about the drinking but good god you'd have to be a monster to, this job, without a snort how could I ever?

KISSINGER.   Ford's not really thinking about Haig, is he?

NIXON.   Haig?

KISSINGER.   He couldn't. It's ludicrous.

NIXON.   Mm.

KISSINGER.   Preposterous.

NIXON.   Of course.

KISSINGER.   He'd be crazy.

NIXON.   When I drink with Bebe, we. On the *Sequoia.* Sailing the Potomac. It gets nostalgic sometimes. Cherished memories. He's got some doozies. Me, too. I have so many. So many good memories.

KISSINGER.   Mmm.

NIXON.   That's why I drink with Bebe. We usually get raucous. That's why I don't drink with Pat, by-the-by. My god. Still, I've got a lot of good memories. No regrets.

KISSINGER.   Mm.

NIXON.   No, I don't think Ford's thinking of Haig.

KISSINGER.   It would be crazy. I do think you should talk to him.

NIXON.   Talk to Ford.

KISSINGER.   Yes.

NIXON.   About you.

KISSINGER.   Make it clear what would be lost if —

NIXON.   Henry, please. Let that go for now. One memory. Growing up. Used to sing this hymn. *(Sings.)* "A mighty Fortress is our God." You know it? Oh. Of course not. Sing it with me anyway.

KISSINGER.   I never sing.

NIXON.   Just this once, its a hymn. A mighty fortress is our God. Go ahead, just that much. It won't kill you.

NIXON and KISSINGER.   *(Sing.)* "A mighty fortress is our God."

NIXON.   Then, um, "A something deep and something." *(Falters.)* Can't remember it. *(Pause.)* What about you? You must have some something. Growing up in Dusseldorf or wherever.

KISSINGER.   Furth.

NIXON.   Fleeing the Nazis and all that stuff.

KISSINGER.   I suppose I do.

NIXON.   Tell one to me. I don't know much about you really. Tell me a nice memory.

KISSINGER.   Well. When we moved to New York.

NIXON.   From Germany.

KISSINGER.   Yes, we fled the, as you said. I was twelve. I was exploring our neighborhood, I was exploring Washington Heights and got a little lost. I looked up and saw four blond-haired boys coming toward me. I stopped. Should I cross the street or just turn and run? Then I remembered I was in America. They passed me, talking and laughing. I was in America, I was safe.

NIXON.   You've never told me that story.

KISSINGER.   No.

NIXON.   I'm touched. It's touching.

KISSINGER.   I've come such a distance. Sometimes I stare in the mirror. What's happening behind those eyes? I'm astonished. Mystified. I like it.

NIXON.   I don't stare in the mirror much. I did on the way up. I did at the height of my. At the height, I'd talk to myself in the mirror. "You sly dog," I'd say. "You never thought you'd get this far." And we'd share a secret smile. But then I fell. I fell like Satan tossed from Heaven.

KISSINGER.   It's the great American story: Requited Ambition. The son of a grocer and an immigrant boy rise to the highest levels of power, change the world.

NIXON.   I suppose. If it'd ended a few months sooner: Happy Ending.

KISSINGER.   A happy story, you keep it going, becomes a tragedy. Tragedy becomes farce.

NIXON.   I set myself up. Ambitious people like us, Henry, once we reach our goal, we should just blow our brains out.

KISSINGER.   So you get elected, you kill yourself. You miss Moscow, China, the Arms Pact, all of it.

NIXON.   There's the catch. You don't know when to kill yourself until it's too late. By the time you figure it out, the moment has passed.... Here's a memory for us both. Meeting Chairman Mao! Gongs sounding, throngs cheering. Zhou being inscrutable all over the place.

KISSINGER.   That was a moment.

NIXON.   Mao. I've never, honestly Henry.

KISSINGER.   Mao. Mao was —

NIXON.   He.

KISSINGER.   Yes.

NIXON.   I've met a lot of great men.

KISSINGER.   I agree.

NIXON.   He.

KISSINGER.   He had an aura.

NIXON.   That's it exactly. An aura. You, in his presence, you *felt* ...

KISSINGER.   I could see how he lead 800 million in revolution.

NIXON.   Oh, yes.

KISSINGER.   The presence.

NIXON.   He did that, the uh, very long hike.

KISSINGER.   The Long March.

NIXON.   My god. I think of myself as a world leader, but. Be him for me.

KISSINGER.   Mr. President, it's late. It's been a difficult —

NIXON.   Just be him. Like you did Brezhnev.

KISSINGER.   — evening.

NIXON.   The Imperial City. Big statues of jade and rosewood. Dragons on the bedposts. Okay. We're led to the Great Hall. Opulence, Henry. Thousands of years of opulence. Carpets thick as thieves. Doors two stories high. And there he sits. "Chairman Mao. The honor of your presence is overwhelming." Then my interpreter says, "Fen Mao shen syin chr he mu gwan lyang!" And Mao says …

KISSINGER-AS-MAO. We are —

NIXON. No. You have to do the Chinese. Mao talks in Chinese.

KISSINGER-AS-MAO. Wǒmén hèn gáusyìng nén yu wǒmén mei gwó de péng you jyàn myàn.

NIXON. No. We're not capturing … it's…. Let's try it again. See if you can get you know. Okay. I enter. *(Drunkenly game, Kissinger becomes Mao. He speaks Chinese as some kind of outsize Samurai warrior. Nixon mimes his words as best he can with superfluous hand gestures.)* Chairman Mao. The honor of your presence is overwhelming.

KISSINGER-AS-MAO. Wǒmén hèn gáusyìng nén yu wǒmén mei gwó de péng you jyàn myàn.

NIXON. We feel this meeting is the first step in a long and harmonious exchange between our two lands.

KISSINGER-AS-MAO. Wo shr lín yáng, ni ye shr lín yáng.

NIXON. … Yes. Or rather you are the dragon, we are the tiger. But the dragon and the tiger can run together.

KISSINGER-AS-MAO. Lyang gwó jr jèn je yin èu túng de jèn jr li lyàn.

NIXON. I have traveled far. I have traveled far to learn from the mouth of the honored Chairman Mao.

KISSINGER-AS-MAO. You are yet young, Nixon. You too will make your Long March. You too will make the Long March from Nixon to yourself.

NIXON. Will I survive this March?

KISSINGER-AS-MAO. Many of my friends died on the March. But they died with honor.

NIXON. Boy was he right. It's much longer than I ever suspected. How will it end? Banished from the kingdom of power! Wandering some hellish golf course, waiting to die. Bathed in glory then flung out on the asphalt tarmac of obscurity. So you see?

KISSINGER. Yes … See what?

NIXON. I've got to stay on. I've got to complete my charge. Finish the March.

KISSINGER. I don't see. I don't see at all.

NIXON. You've got to help me.

KISSINGER. What are you saying?

NIXON. It's bigger than all of us.

KISSINGER. It's. Have you been listening?

NIXON. America loves a fighter.

KISSINGER. America's, you've got to.

NIXON. It's clear. It's so clear.

KISSINGER. Clear?

NIXON. Once you give up power, it's gone. You're out, finished. As long as I'm in power, I've got a chance, I've got somewhere to fight from.

KISSINGER. Fight for what? Everything's gone to hell.

NIXON. Better a ruler in Hell, Henry, than a servant in Heaven. If I've learned anything, I've learned that.

KISSINGER. Look. Wait. No. Our last visit to Russia. You and Brezhnev, out at his dacha.

NIXON. With the hunting.

KISSINGER. Yes. And after. He spoke to you. Alone.

NIXON. He wanted, just he and I. He wanted to —

KISSINGER. I know what he wanted to say.

NIXON. He wanted to tell me —

KISSINGER-AS-BREZHNEV. Nixon! I knew you would make a hunter. I knew it.

NIXON. He didn't say anything like that.

KISSINGER-AS-BREZHNEV. Truthfully, I almost never catch anything. So today is not so different. It's the hunt itself I love. The actual killing — peah.

NIXON. *(Enters into game.)* We almost, I damn near got that one.

KISSINGER-AS-BREZHNEV. We Soviets, Nixon, we love the outdoors. A country so vast, so unconquerable. It is sublime. I'm sorry about your troubles.

NIXON. Oh, it's, um. I'll easily overcome the.

KISSINGER-AS-BREZHNEV. I so love it out here, away from the corridors of power. Everything such a tawny green. Did I ever tell you what happened with Svoboda? Oh, Nixon, what a story! So. '68. Prague Spring. Our tanks roll in, BAM, movement crushed. We take Dubcek into custody. Bring him to the Kremlin. Czechoslovakia's left in turmoil. We don't know what to do about the whole thing. You crush a national movement, now what? I schedule a chat with Svoboda, hoping to work something out. You know. You know him?

NIXON. I know the name.

KISSINGER-AS-BREZHNEV. Went from apricot farmer to soldier to President of the Republic of Czechoslovakia. A true believer in the rights of the common man. Drink. He comes to the Kremlin. To discuss. We sit, very civilized. Much like you and I now. I know what I want, I'm holding all the cards. I look across the table, complacent in my fat power. "Svoboda," I say, tapping his file, "from here on out you do just as I decide." And here, Nixon, here, Ludvik Svoboda, a two-bit functionary from Eastern Europe, throws his Lenin medal to the table, reaches to his pocket, and suddenly is holding a revolver.

NIXON. In the Kremlin?

KISSINGER-AS-BREZHNEV. But Svoboda didn't want to shoot me. This man, he presses the barrel of the gun to his own neck. *(Kissinger points Nixon's finger toward Nixon's neck.)* "Release my friend Dubcek, or I scatter my brains."

NIXON. "Release my friend Dubcek, or I scatter my brains."

KISSINGER-AS-BREZHNEV. You see Nixon, I can't call his bluff. I can't. He kills himself, who will believe it? No one. The world will think we murdered him. The world will think we murdered Ludvik Svoboda in cold blood in the Kremlin.

NIXON. What happened?

KISSINGER-AS-BREZHNEV. I gave him Dubcek. Otherwise it's public relations disaster.

NIXON. Ludvik Svoboda. I had no idea.

KISSINGER-AS-BREZHNEV. Many heroic acts go unheralded. They are still heroic. When I looked into Svoboda's eyes, eyes green as this field, I knew he meant it. I knew I'd met a man who placed his convictions far above his own person.

NIXON. You think I should resign.

KISSINGER-AS-BREZHNEV. One day a scientist will write the equations of politics. Power equals Force times Time. We'd like the personal to be a factor in the equation, but ultimately, it is no factor. Khrushchev was a friend, a mentor, a father to me. But my love for him was not enough to counter the great forces of history. So I ousted him. Now the equations of politics are turned against you, my beloved Nixon.

NIXON.   Force times Time.

KISSINGER-AS-BREZHNEV.   It will be painful. I know that. I've seen what loss of power can do. But then again, how many chances does one have to perform a heroic act? A selfless act that serves one's nation?

NIXON.   Very impressive, Henry. Had me going. "Tawny green fields." "Heroic act." Yes, nicely done. When you came in, you know what I was hoping? I was hoping for the smallest of things — I was hoping you'd try to talk me out of resigning. Just one little attempt, one little gesture, out of ... respect? But no. Brandy?

KISSINGER.   It's getting late.

NIXON.   I got these yesterday. You might be interested. Transcripts.

KISSINGER.   Of...?

NIXON.   J. Edgar never took the tap off. He took all the others off, but not yours.

KISSINGER.   Transcripts of my...?

NIXON.   Read what you said.

KISSINGER.   *(As he reads.)* These are. This is. Taken completely out of context. But this, I didn't say anything — oh. Oh. Part of staff camaraderie is to ridicule you. I had to ingratiate myself. You know how it's played.

NIXON.   Do I?

KISSINGER.   You're getting sidetracked with irrelevancies.

NIXON.   You're missing a larger point here. About the transcripts.

KISSINGER.   I didn't mean any of this.

NIXON.   Look at that one.

KISSINGER.   *(Reads.)* This was recorded?

NIXON.   ...

KISSINGER.   This was recorded?!

NIXON.   ...

KISSINGER.   This. You've. Where're the tapes?

NIXON.   That's it, Henry. That's just it. You see, in the tapes, the subpoenaed tapes, I talk about these. Haldeman and I, it's discussed. The tap on you.

KISSINGER.   But they have nothing to do with your whole mess.

NIXON.   Yeah, but somebody thinks they might, they'll want to hear 'em. I go meddling with 'em, say erase a few minutes, well, as we know, everybody screams bloody murder.

KISSINGER.   The Bureau's got them?

NIXON.   It does.

KISSINGER.   So no one can get to them. So Gray can fix this.

NIXON.   Gray? Gray doesn't know me from Grover Cleveland.

KISSINGER.   But he can fix it.

NIXON.   Why, Henry? I don't know the guy. It's not like when J. Edgar was alive. I can't just call up FBI and say whatever. There's no percentage in it for him. I'm out.

KISSINGER.   But, this gets out. This gets out. This is highly confidential government business.

NIXON.   You're right.

KISSINGER.   This is not for the public to know.

NIXON.   Yes. I see.

KISSINGER.   IT WOULD BE A CRIME.

NIXON.   Your work —

KISSINGER.   DOESN'T HE UNDERSTAND?

NIXON.   — it would —

KISSINGER.   WHAT DOES HE, HE. I'm…. You've got to talk to him.

NIXON.   I have.

KISSINGER.   Again. You've, don't you see, it's *our* reputation. Our place in the books.

NIXON.   *(Wanders to the record player.)* He won't see reason. He's adamant.

KISSINGER.   No. No, no. We've got to. There's got to be some. How can we do this?

NIXON.   Henry. If I'm President, if the impeachment thing goes away, then it's okay. If I'm President, Gray comes through.

I've got to be President.

KISSINGER. "If the impeachment thing goes away?" What on earth can make that happen?

NIXON. You're the genius.

KISSINGER. You can't stay President. It's impossible.

NIXON. Perhaps some Ravel. *"Rhapsodie Espagnole?"*

KISSINGER. Somewhere, stuffed in Hoover's old mattress is a spool of brown tape that can *tarnish* ... irredeemably ...

NIXON. You.

KISSINGER. Yes.

NIXON. And what the fuck are you going to do about it? Now look here, Henry. I pulled you off the Harvard shit pile, I gave you power you never dreamed of, I made you a world figure. Now, here, at this historic moment, at least you can fight for me. And for you. I'm President, those tapes disappear.

KISSINGER. One must base one's decisions on basic principles. In the case of reputation, one must not imperil actual power —

NIXON. There's a real possibility Ford might choose Haig.

KISSINGER. Haig?

NIXON. If you were Ford, you'd want to show you're your own man.

KISSINGER. Ford might choose Haig?

NIXON. Al's probably lobbying right this minute.

KISSINGER. You're saying keeping you in power —

NIXON. Keeps *you* in power.

KISSINGER. And if you're in power, you'll fight to prevent the tapes from getting out.

NIXON. How do we do it?

KISSINGER. The tapes will remain —

NIXON. *Yes.* How do we do it?

KISSINGER. To block impeachment in the Senate you need thirty-four votes, and you've got...?

NIXON. Ten.

KISSINGER. Ten?!

NIXON. Six.

KISSINGER. Six?! You need twenty-eight Senators?

NIXON.   They change their minds in herds. Even Goldwater for chrissakes. Judas-priest.

KISSINGER.   Has FBI got stuff on twenty-eight Senators?

NIXON.   That stuff's no good.

KISSINGER.   Of course it's no good, but can you use it?

NIXON.   They could beat it. Claim political motivation. Which, let's face it.

KISSINGER.   It's hopeless. You'd need an international crisis.

NIXON.   That's what I was thinking.

KISSINGER.   ... You were thinking you'd need an international crises?

NIXON.   Don't you think so? Look at it. It's my only hope.

KISSINGER.   But. It's. It's too obvious for one thing.

NIXON.   We'll do it subtlety.

KISSINGER.   You're being forced to resign so you provoke a crisis.

NIXON.   *I* don't provoke a crisis.

KISSINGER.   What? *I* provoke a crisis?

NIXON.   Don't you get it? Brezhnev, Chou, Hussein, they're our friends. They're our base of support.

KISSINGER.   You want them to provoke a crisis?

NIXON.   One of them.

KISSINGER.   Well, which one?

NIXON.   Dammit, are you going to work with me on this? How many international crises have you and I dealt with? What's one more?

KISSINGER.   Say we try it. How would it work?

NIXON.   All right. You'd go to say, Israel and say, "Golda, here's the deal."

KISSINGER.   Madame Prime Minister, here's the deal.

NIXON.   Then you —

KISSINGER.   No. "Madame Prime Minister, here's the deal."

NIXON.   What?

KISSINGER.   What's she say? *(Pause.)*

NIXON-AS-GOLDA MEIR.   What deal?

KISSINGER.   President Nixon has been a good friend to you.

NIXON-AS-GOLDA MEIR.   What do you want?

KISSINGER.   The President is in grave difficulty. We feel that if certain ... tensions latent in the Middle East situation were to become more apparent, the American Congress might better appreciate President Nixon's worth.

NIXON-AS-GOLDA MEIR. You want me to start a war to save Nixon?

KISSINGER. We don't want you to risk anything of the sort. We just want to point out, in view of the President's great friendship and support of Israel, that if you were planning any provocative action vis-à-vis any of your neighbors, perhaps your time-table could be moved up. That's all.

NIXON-AS-GOLDA MEIR. What kind of Jew are you?

KISSINGER. I don't think Israel's the one to go to.

NIXON. No. A flare-up in the Mideast isn't going to do it anyway. People've gotten used to it.

KISSINGER. We could get Brezhnev to attack somebody small. But ...

NIXON. The reactions on both sides ...

KISSINGER. Not much margin for error. We need something ... it would be good if it didn't directly involve the U.S., that way, if it gets out of control, you know, who cares?

NIXON. Right. Right. But it'll have to be pretty big. We've got to think big. *(They think.)* How 'bout — no. No, that's stupid.

KISSINGER. We talk to CIA, we talk to ... *(Hesitates.)*

NIXON. Colby?

KISSINGER. No. We talk to.... We're not being recorded now, are we?

NIXON. You think I'm trying to destroy us?

KISSINGER. We talk to ... the appropriate person.

NIXON. I'm with you.

KISSINGER. And we say, "Do such-and-such at such-and-such a place."

NIXON. Secretly.

KISSINGER. Secretly, yes.

NIXON. And such-and-such is some —

KISSINGER. I have it.

NIXON. — some very dire —

KISSINGER. All we need, this is perfect, is some very provocative act along the Chinese-Soviet border.

NIXON. Yes.

KISSINGER. Something, um ...

NIXON. A provincial mayor gets assassinated kind of thing.

KISSINGER. Right.

NIXON. Right.

KISSINGER. It looks like the Russians are behind it.

NIXON. Exactly.

KISSINGER. China reacts, Brezhnev threatens escalation —

NIXON. Back and forth. Up and up.

KISSINGER. We tell both sides what's going to happen.

NIXON. Then, sunuvagun, it does.

KISSINGER. They each think we're with them.

NIXON. We play 'em like banjos.

KISSINGER. Everybody's tense. This conflict, so far away, so uncontrollable. Apt to grow exponentially. A real chance of global nuclear exchange.

NIXON. A world on the brink.

KISSINGER. Who can prevent World War? Who has the Power and Prestige and *Trust* of the Soviet Union and China? Who?

NIXON. Me.

KISSINGER. The one man on the *globe* who can reconcile all parties. The one man who can restore peace.

NIXON. Me.

KISSINGER. Bungled cover-ups will seem so paltry. Inconsequential. The Congress, the courts will be embarrassed to pursue such trivia.

NIXON. Me.

KISSINGER. So, it plays out kind of, um. *(As if responding to reporters on the Capitol steps.)* "I, I really can't speculate on what the President will say this evening. I do know he's been in contact with several world leaders. I've shared my thoughts with him, but, no, he's kept us all in the dark about what he'll be saying tonight."

NIXON. "My fellow Americans." What am I, LBJ? "Fellow citizens." No. "Loyal subjects?"

KISSINGER. Fellow Americans.

NIXON.   "Fellow Americans, a world in crisis finds no easy solutions. Many of you tonight are deeply troubled by the tensions in Northern China. You fear that events are spinning beyond control and feel the shadow of nuclear war approaching." That's good.

KISSINGER.   Shadow of war's good. You need more 'here it is.'

NIXON.   Um. "Even more troubling is the fact that this crisis comes at a time when my own Presidency is under attack here at home."

KISSINGER.   Good.

NIXON.   "I suffer no delusions about the extent to which my personal plight has divided this nation. But, citizens of America, I am yet President of the United States."

KISSINGER.   Excellent. Then you get in 'spoken at length with Brezhnev, Zhou-en-Lai, who've requested your personal involvement.'

NIXON.   Right. And then, "Secretary of State Kissinger," something, "also believes ..." Um.

KISSINGER.   ... the strength of your friendship with both countries is required for and so on.

NIXON.   Yes. Exactly. Then I end it on a, um, you know ...

KISSINGER.   "But to do this, I'll need your support. The support of each of you ..."

NIXON.   "... no matter your opinion of me personally, I ask you to reach into your hearts and to afford me ..."

KISSINGER.   "... a brief space of time to devote myself unflaggingly to the crisis in Manchuria."

NIXON.   "In return for your forbearance, beyond my gratitude I pledge that once the crisis has passed, once the crisis has passed ... I will resign." *(They are surprised.)*

KISSINGER.   My god.

NIXON.   "And the United States of America can turn to healing itself."

KISSINGER.   That's it! You resign then.

NIXON.   Christ, I'm a genius.

KISSINGER.   You save the world, then one final gracious bow.

NIXON.   What court would pursue me?

KISSINGER.   A few weeks of empty legalities, then it's forgotten.

NIXON.   I'm off. Scot-free.

KISSINGER.   The resignation becomes a heroic act.

NIXON.   The great warrior quitting the field.

KISSINGER.   After my role in such a thing, Ford could never let me go.

NIXON.   "Men of France!"

KISSINGER.   Nothing could stand in my way.

NIXON.   All right, Henry. We've got the scenario. How do we set it going?

KISSINGER.   Like we said.

NIXON.   Some dinky assassination in Irkutsk's not going to make middle America pee it's pants.

KISSINGER.   Well ...

NIXON.   We need something with bravado. Pizzazz.

KISSINGER.   Sure.

NIXON.   You think Ike did things by half-measures?

KISSINGER.   So what do we need?

NIXON.   Burning villages! Rape, pillage.

KISSINGER.   We can't just do that. We've got to ... maybe air-drop, I don't know.

NIXON.   Bad chemicals or something.

KISSINGER.   Yes. Or why not just. Bombs?

NIXON.   Bombs?

KISSINGER.   We've always been good at —

NIXON.   We don't even have to drop any. We put a plane up there with Soviet markings. The Chinese shoot it down, slam! Everybody's on red alert.

KISSINGER.   *Then* an assassination.

NIXON.   Then an assassination. Right.

KISSINGER.   The press starts talking Archduke Ferdinand.

NIXON.   Maybe an incident in Berlin as well.

KISSINGER.   The imagination runs riot.

NIXON.   Bam! Bam!

KISSINGER.   We time the incidents according to the press.

NIXON.   Provincial mayors dropping like flies.

KISSINGER. If it comes to it, we detonate a small one somewhere.

NIXON. Let 'em know they've crossed me. Let 'em know they've pushed me too far. Cities crumble. Nations catch fire.

KISSINGER. They'll never recover.

NIXON. Then let 'em impeach me, let the hippies and the Harvard judges and the pinko congressmen and the fag reporters impeach me with the world on fire.

KISSINGER. Destruction. Destruction everywhere.

NIXON. Bombs from the sky. Kablooie!

KISSINGER. Novosibirsk.

NIXON. Bombs from the sky. Kablooie!

KISSINGER. Shanghai.

NIXON. Bombs from the sky. Kablooie!

KISSINGER. Mozambique.

NIXON. Kablooie!

KISSINGER. Brisbane.

NIXON. Kablooie!

KISSINGER. Hong Kong.

NIXON. Kablooie!

KISSINGER. London!

NIXON. Bombers blacken the skies. People think the sun's going down.

KISSINGER. Then the bombs fall.

NIXON. They fall like leaves. Like hail stones.

KISSINGER. Like ashes.

NIXON. Bombs fall like night. A night of fire. A snow of embers.

KISSINGER. Rice farmers harvest little bits of their friends.

NIXON. People everywhere open their mouths, but their tongues lie dead of shock.

KISSINGER. And then, you step in!

NIXON. "Fellow Americans."

KISSINGER. Order is restored. You're a hero.

NIXON. *(Picks up phone.)* Get me Brezhnev. No, let's not let him in on it. Get me CIA.

KISSINGER. Let me talk to them.

NIXON.   Yeah. Who is this? Blow the fuckers up.

KISSINGER.   *(Grabs phone.)* Blow them up. Whoever. Whatever. Whenever.

NIXON.   *(Grabs phone.)* Start with small fuckers, then blow up bigger and bigger fuckers.

KISSINGER.   *(Grabs phone.)* Those're the orders, pal. From the top.

NIXON.   *(Grabs phone.)* The very, very top. The President of the United States. *(Hangs up. Somber. Time passes.)* *(Nixon gazes out front.)* It's lovely, isn't it?

KISSINGER.   ... The...?

NIXON.   If you didn't know it was real, you'd think it was phony. You'd think it was a painting. What's that way out there, Henry? Some famous pass? Some famous mountain? Towering above the land of the great Khan. This wall has kept away enemies for twenty-three hundred years. What is it out there, Henry? What do you see? *(Pause.)*

KISSINGER.   I see the plains of Tun-shen stretching out to the Gobi.

NIXON.   Imagine the power.

KISSINGER.   Yes.

NIXON.   It must've felt good to give that command. "Build a wall." That's all you'd have to say. Next day, *this'd* be begun. How long is it?

KISSINGER.   Fourteen hundred miles.

NIXON.   Feel this. The dust of dynasties. If I were the Emperor Huang-Ti, those years ago, I'd build this wall. I'd build this wall so strong, none would dream of attacking me. I would build this wall and my kingdom would be secure.

KISSINGER.   It's late, sir. We should head back.

NIXON.   At this moment, standing here, gazing over the plains of Tun-shen, right at this precise moment, I'm the most powerful man ever. For just this ... moment. *(Nixon returns to the present.)**

*This section between the asterisks was cut in the original Off-Broadway Production.

How many did we kill, Henry?

KISSINGER.   When's this?

NIXON.   You know. Over all. How many? In Viet Nam, say. Since I'm President.

KISSINGER.   Fifty-five thousand.

NIXON.   No. Since I became President.

KISSINGER.   Oh. Twenty-one thousand.

NIXON.   How many Viet Cong?

KISSINGER.   Two-hundred eighty-thousand.

NIXON.   North Vietnamese army?

KISSINGER.   One-hundred twenty-thousand.

NIXON.   South Vietnamese army?

KISSINGER.   One-hundred forty-thousand.

NIXON.   Civilians?

KISSINGER.   One-hundred eighty-thousand.

NIXON.   The Cambodian bombings?

KISSINGER.   Eighteen thousand.

NIXON.   And in Laos?

KISSINGER.   Laos? About twenty thousand.

NIXON.   Chile?

KISSINGER.   But these aren't —

NIXON.   Chile?

KISSINGER.   Twelve thousand.

NIXON.   About eight-hundred thousand so far. Eight-hundred thousand and one, counting Allende. Then there's Kent State. Eight-hundred thousand and five.

KISSINGER.   Mr. President.

NIXON.   Eight-hundred thousand and five all together. Eight-hundred thousand and five dead on my watch.

KISSINGER.   A world leader makes decisions.

NIXON.   Still. Eight-hundred thousand dead. Kablooie. Now I resign? Now I spend the rest of my days wading in a swimming pool of blood? There're times. Muh. In the army they've got it easy. Someone leaves a gun in a drawer. I don't have a gun.

KISSINGER.   Sir, you've got to —

NIXON.   Oh, Dear god, I need your help. I feel like I should be asking forgiveness, but I don't feel like I've done anything

46

wrong. They gave me so much power, why are they surprised I used it? And where were You? Where the fuck have You been? Here I am, on my *knees*. Just to get You to help me realize that sometimes the courageous thing isn't to struggle on. Sometimes, it takes more courage, more honor to, to throw in the towel. Can't you help me realize that? But then what, Henry? Then I'll need Him more than ever. You see, I can make the speeches. I can thank people and say, you know, the things that have to be said. I can do that. But after, I've got to climb the ramp into the helicopter. To take me away. Climb those metal stairs fighting the roar of the engines. One step after another. Nothing but a handrail. And then, at the top, I'll have to turn to the crowd. I'll have to say good-bye with dignity. Good-bye to all my power. Good-bye to all my joy. Good-bye to all my pain. Good-bye to all I've ever been. How on God's green earth will I be able to do it?

KISSINGER.   Sir. Sir.

NIXON.   I need You to let me know it'll be all right, if I can just make it up that ramp. Please. Just let me know that. If I can just.

KISSINGER.   Sir. It'll be okay.

NIXON.   God. Why won't You let me know it'll be all right? Goddamnit, why won't You just tell me that?

KISSINGER.   It'll be all right. *(Kissinger touches him on the arm. Nixon pulls away in fury.)*

NIXON.   Sorry, Henry. I'm. I.

KISSINGER.   It's. Sir.

NIXON.   I didn't mean for.

KISSINGER.   I should be leaving.

NIXON.   It's the strain. The. It's unbearable. It's a miracle.

KISSINGER.   You've withstood. Considering.

NIXON.   I'll need a speech. A resignation speech to the nation. I suppose the boys in the back've already written something.

KISSINGER.   An outline. Just in case.

NIXON.   Also a good-bye to the staff. I'll write that. To all those who've. Stuck by.

KISSINGER.   Of course.

NIXON. All those who've, in the face of so much. Especially Julie, Henry. She's been such a soldier.

KISSINGER. Yes. Yes, I know.

NIXON. I wish I could.... There're some things I wish I could say to her. All she's done. Gone through. I just don't know if I. I should say, Julie. I let you down. I let you make all those speeches. All over hell's half-acre, telling everybody what a good man I am. I let you tell people I hadn't done things. When you were a little girl. Four, five? After I gave the Checkers speech, just after. I came home, I thought it was a dud, I thought my career was over. I was angry, I snapped at Pat, everyone trying to tell me it'd gone so well. I came into the house and slammed the door and there you were with Checkers in your arms. You looked up at me with the biggest smile. "Daddy! You said Checkers on TV!" I thought my heart would. Break.

Julie. I did do things. I did. And if I let you go saying over and over that I hadn't — it's just that nobody ever showed me that much love before.

I didn't know how to tell you that your dad was a bum. I was afraid you'd lose all respect for your old man. That was something I couldn't. Julie. Could you. Could you tell me ...

KISSINGER. Father. I've always respected you. I'll always love you.

NIXON. All right. Now what'll I tell those bastards? Friends. Dear, dear, friends. We think that when someone dear to us leaves, we think when we lose an election, we think that when we suffer a defeat, that all has ended.

KISSINGER. Mr. President. *(Slow fade-in of helicopter noise.)*

NIXON. Not true. It is only a beginning, always. The young must know it, the old must know it. It must always sustain us, because the greatness comes not when things go always good for you —

KISSINGER. Mr. President.

NIXON. — but greatness comes and you are really tested when you take some knocks, some disappointments, when sadness comes.

KISSINGER. What about the tapes, Mr. President? *(Add un-*

derlying grating drone to helicopter.)

NIXON.   Because only if you have been in the deepest valley can you ever know how magnificent it is to be on the highest mountain. *(He seems to be ascending the steps to the helicopter.)*

KISSINGER.   Can you keep the tapes!? Mr. President! Come back! The tapes! *(But he is lost in darkness and his continued pleas are swallowed by the roar of the engine. Noise swells to a deafening level. Richard Nixon, standing atop the stairs, turns and determinedly gives his final wave, complete with rueful, forced smile/frown. Blackout. Cut sound.)*

END OF PLAY

PROPERTY LIST

Rolled up transcripts (NIXON)
Decanter of brandy (NIXON)
Brandy glasses (NIXON)
Telephone

SOUND EFFECTS

Fade in: helicoptor, approaching;
              add drone;
              then swelling of sound

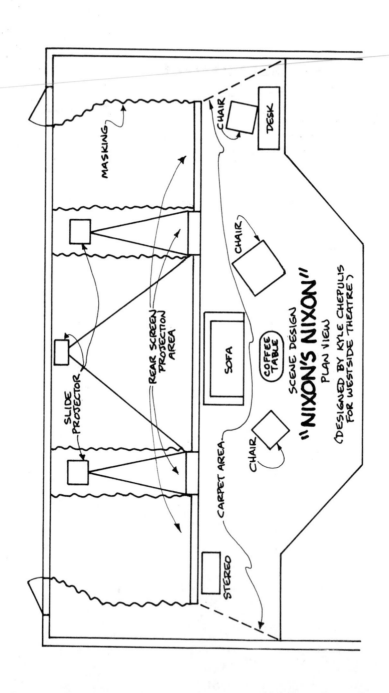

SCENE DESIGN
"NIXON'S NIXON"
PLAN VIEW

(DESIGNED BY KYLE CHEPULIS
FOR WESTSIDE THEATRE)

NEW PLAYS

★ **CLOSER by Patrick Marber.** Winner of the 1998 Olivier Award for Best Play and the 1999 New York Drama Critics Circle Award for Best Foreign Play. Four lives intertwine over the course of four and a half years in this densely plotted, stinging look at modern love and betrayal. "CLOSER is a sad, savvy, often funny play that casts a steely, unblinking gaze at the world of relationships ... CLOSER does not merely hold your attention; it burrows into you." *–New York Magazine* "A powerful, darkly funny play about the cosmic collision between the sun of love and the comet of desire." *–Newsweek Magazine* [2M, 2W] ISBN: 0-8222-1722-8

★ **THE MOST FABULOUS STORY EVER TOLD by Paul Rudnick.** A stage manager, headset and prompt book at hand, brings the house lights to half, then dark, and cues the creation of the world. Throughout the play, she's in control of everything. In other words, she's either God, or she thinks she is. "Line by line, Mr. Rudnick may be the funniest writer for the stage in the United States today ... One-liners, epigrams, withering put-downs and flashing repartee: These are the candles that Mr. Rudnick lights instead of cursing the darkness ... a testament to the virtues of laughing ... and in laughter, there is something like the memory of Eden." *–The NY Times* "Funny it is ... consistently, rapaciously, deliriously ... easily the funniest play in town." *–Variety* [4M, 5W] ISBN: 0-8222-1720-1

★ **A DOLL'S HOUSE by Henrik Ibsen, adapted by Frank McGuinness.** Winner of the 1997 Tony Award for Best Revival. "New, raw, gut-twisting and gripping. Easily the hottest drama this season." *–USA Today* "Bold, brilliant and alive." *–The Wall Street Journal* "A thunderclap of an evening that takes your breath away." *–Time Magazine* [4M, 4W, 2 boys] ISBN: 0-8222-1636-1

★ **THE HERBAL BED by Peter Whelan.** The play is based on actual events which occurred in Stratford-upon-Avon in the summer of 1613, when William Shakespeare's elder daughter was publicly accused of having a sexual liaison with a married neighbor and family friend. "In his probing new play, THE HERBAL BED ... Peter Whelan muses about a sidelong event in the life of Shakespeare's family and creates a finely textured tapestry of love and lies in the early 17th-century Stratford." *–The NY Times* "It is a first rate drama with interesting moral issues of truth and expediency." *–The NY Post* [5M, 3W] ISBN: 0-8222-1675-2

★ **SNAKEBIT by David Marshall Grant.** A study of modern friendship when put to the test. "... a rather smart and absorbing evening of water-cooler theater, the intimate sort of Off-Broadway experience that has you picking apart the recognizable characters long after the curtain calls." *– The NY Times* "Off-Broadway keeps on presenting us with compelling reasons for going to the theater. The latest is SNAKEBIT, David Marshall Grant's smart new comic drama about being thirtysomething and losing one's way in life." *–The NY Daily News* [3M, 1W] ISBN: 0-8222-1724-4

★ **A QUESTION OF MERCY by David Rabe.** The Obie Award-winning playwright probes the sensitive and controversial issue of doctor-assisted suicide in the age of AIDS in this poignant drama. "There are many devastating ironies in Mr. Rabe's beautifully considered, piercingly clear-eyed work ..." *–The NY Times* "With unsettling candor and disturbing insight, the play arouses pity and understanding of a troubling subject ... Rabe's provocative tale is an affirmation of dignity that rings clear and true." *–Variety* [6M, 1W] ISBN: 0-8222-1643-4

★ **DiMLY PERCEIVED THREATS TO THE SYSTEM by Jon Klein.** Reality and fantasy overlap with hilarious results as this unforgettable family attempts to survive the nineties. "Here's a play whose point about fractured families goes to the heart, mind – and ears." *–The Washington Post* "... an end-of-the millennium comedy about a family on the verge of a nervous breakdown ... Trenchant and hilarious ..." *–The Baltimore Sun* [2M, 4W] ISBN: 0-8222-1677-9

DRAMATISTS PLAY SERVICE, INC.
440 Park Avenue South, New York, NY 10016 212-683-8960 Fax 212-213-1539
postmaster@dramatists.com www.dramatists.com

NEW PLAYS

★ **AS BEES IN HONEY DROWN by Douglas Carter Beane.** Winner of the John Gassner Playwriting Award. A hot young novelist finds the subject of his new screenplay in a New York socialite who leads him into the world of *Auntie Mame* and *Breakfast at Tiffany's*, before she takes him for a ride. "A delicious soufflé of a satire … [an] extremely entertaining fable for an age that always chooses image over substance." –*The NY Times* "… A witty assessment of one of the most active and relentless industries in a consumer society … the creation of 'hot' young things, which the media have learned to mass produce with efficiency and zeal." –*The NY Daily News* [3M, 3W, flexible casting] ISBN: 0-8222-1651-5

★ **STUPID KIDS by John C. Russell.** In rapid, highly stylized scenes, the story follows four high-school students as they make their way from first through eighth period and beyond, struggling with the fears, frustrations, and longings peculiar to youth. "In STUPID KIDS … playwright John C. Russell does the opera of adolescence to a T … The stylized teenspeak of STUPID KIDS … suggests that Mr. Russell may have hidden a tape recorder under a desk in study hall somewhere and then scoured the tapes for good quotations … it is the kids' insular, ceaselessly churning world, a pre-adult world of Doritos and libidos, that the playwright seeks to lay bare." –*The NY Times* "STUPID KIDS [is] a sharp-edged … whoosh of teen angst and conformity anguish. It is also very funny." –*NY Newsday* [2M, 2W] ISBN: 0-8222-1698-1

★ **COLLECTED STORIES by Donald Margulies.** From Obie Award-winner Donald Margulies comes a provocative analysis of a student-teacher relationship that turns sour when the protégé becomes a rival. "With his fine ear for detail, Margulies creates an authentic, insular world, and he gives equal weight to the opposing viewpoints of two formidable characters." –*The LA Times* "This is probably Margulies' best play to date …" –*The NY Post* "… always fluid and lively, the play is thick with ideas, like a stock-pot of good stew." –*The Village Voice* [2W] ISBN: 0-8222-1640-X

★ **FREEDOMLAND by Amy Freed.** An overdue showdown between a son and his father sets off fireworks that illuminate the neurosis, rage and anxiety of one family – and of America at the turn of the millennium. "FREEDOMLAND's more obvious links are to *Buried Child* and *Bosoms and Neglect*. Freed, like Guare, is an inspired wordsmith with a gift for surreal touches in situations grounded in familiar and real territory." –*Curtain Up* [3M, 4W] ISBN: 0-8222-1719-8

★ **STOP KISS by Diana Son.** A poignant and funny play about the ways, both sudden and slow, that lives can change irrevocably. "There's so much that is vital and exciting about STOP KISS … you want to embrace this young author and cheer her onto other works … the writing on display here is funny and credible … you also will be charmed by its heartfelt characters and up-to-the-minute humor." –*The NY Daily News* "… irresistibly exciting … a sweet, sad, and enchantingly sincere play." –*The NY Times* [3M, 3W] ISBN: 0-8222-1731-7

★ **THREE DAYS OF RAIN by Richard Greenberg.** The sins of fathers and mothers make for a bittersweet elegy in this poignant and revealing drama. "… a work so perfectly judged it heralds the arrival of a major playwright … Greenberg is extraordinary." –*The NY Daily News* "Greenberg's play is filled with graceful passages that are by turns melancholy, harrowing, and often, quite funny." –*Variety* [2M, 1W] ISBN: 0-8222-1676-0

★ **THE WEIR by Conor McPherson.** In a bar in rural Ireland, the local men swap spooky stories in an attempt to impress a young woman from Dublin who recently moved into a nearby "haunted" house. However, the tables are soon turned when she spins a yarn of her own. "You shed all sense of time at this beautiful and devious new play." –*The NY Times* "Sheer theatrical magic. I have rarely been so convinced that I have just seen a modern classic. Tremendous." –*The London Daily Telegraph* [4M, 1W] ISBN: 0-8222-1706-6

DRAMATISTS PLAY SERVICE, INC.
440 Park Avenue South, New York, NY 10016 212-683-8960 Fax 212-213-1539
postmaster@dramatists.com www.dramatists.com